The Holiday Badass
by John Wesley Adams

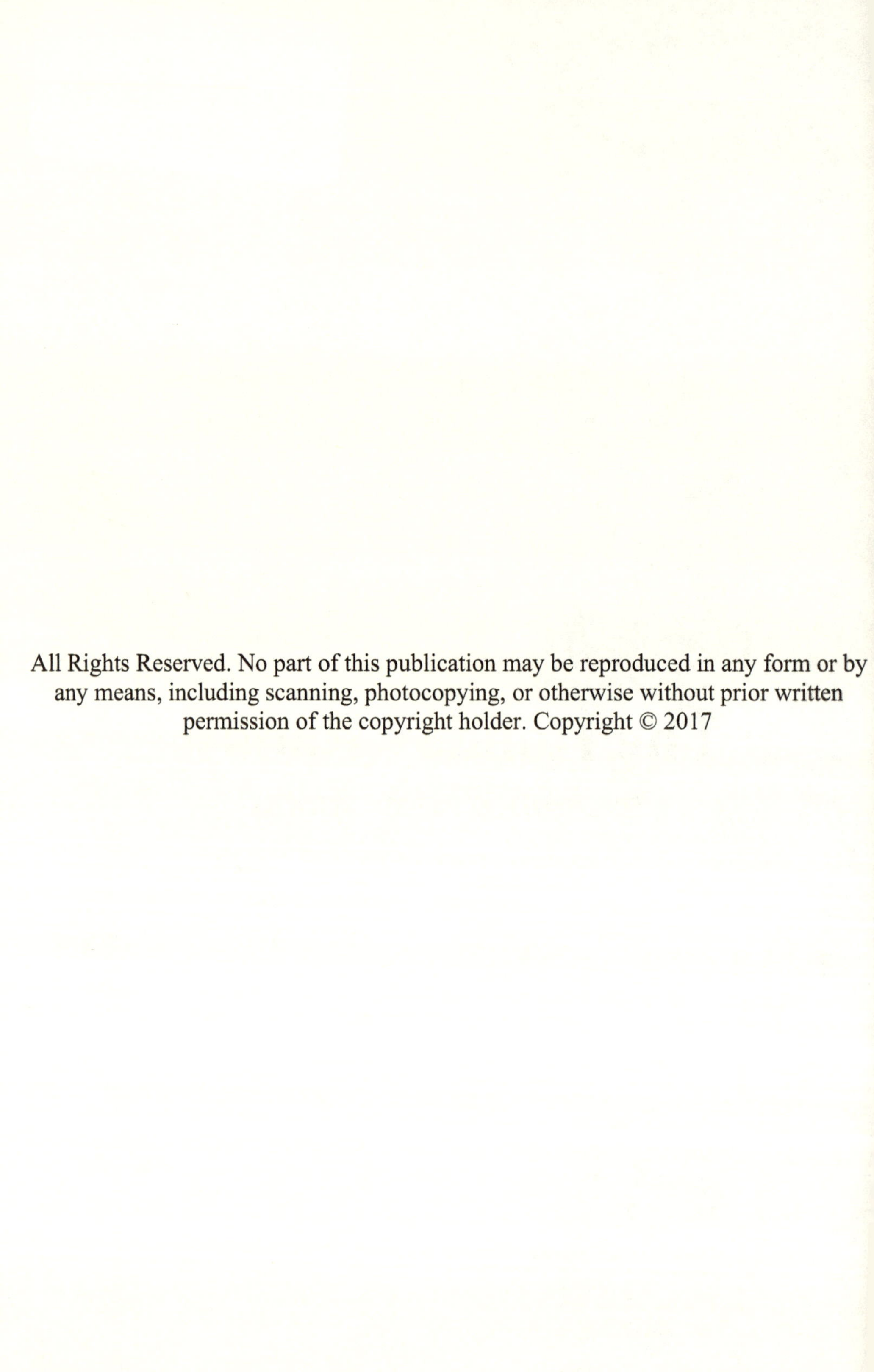

Table of Contents

"The Beautiful Moon" by J.W. Adams

—

Dedicated to

You, The Reader.

Thank you for taking time to listen to what I have to say.

I hope by the time you finish this book,

you will have found the badass within YOU.

--John

Introduction

Holiday Blues

Holiday Blues

We are told by society that Christmas is supposed to be the happiest time of the year. Unfortunately, it is the exact opposite for many of us. Maybe even the sound of cheerful Christmas tunes on the radio can cause us to be irritated or even angry. For others, the feeling is more of a sadness. Maybe we miss our loved ones, maybe we have had a couple really bad Christmases, or maybe our finances mean that we will have to cope with a lean approach to giving presents this year.

No matter the reason, there is always hope that this year is your time to take back the holidays. Don't let the happiest season of the year be your private pity party. Use the strategies in this book to make this a great holiday. You can make this your first BADASS Christmas!

John W. Adams

Introduction to First Edition

It amazes me how cruel we can be to ourselves. We are appalled when we hear a story of a mother cat eating her babies, but many of us do this to ourselves mentally every day. A positive thought will crop up, and we will devour it and smother it with negativity. It's easy for us to excuse this as "just keeping things realistic," but if being realistic were such a virtue, why don't we hear lessons about it? There isn't a single wise teacher, living or dead, who would warn you not to set your hopes too high, and life coaches do not tell their clients that being more cautious is the path to success. While we're on the subject, since when did Jesus teach that being realistic was the best approach?

A counselor or therapist might advise a person to use greater caution when making decisions, but this is only good advice for someone who clearly lacks control over their behavior. Many people suffer from periods of extreme over-confidence, but if you are reading this, you need completely different advice.

I know exactly where you are coming from. Like you, I always thought I was missing something. Everyone else seemed so confident. They were sure of their decisions and I was always amazed how easily they brushed it off when they were wrong.

Then, bam! It hit me! What I suffered from was TOO much thinking before doing.

These blissful jerks who always seem so confident in themselves because they don't waste precious time wondering what they want. They KNOW what they want because they listen to their gut. Now they can spend their mental powers of problem solving to figure out HOW they can get what they want. Never IF, just HOW.

Think of all of the non-divine, noteworthy contributions made by ordinary people with unrealistic ideas. We try so hard to stay realistic in a world that celebrates those who scoff at realism. Where is the logic? The payoff we get from this self-defeated behavior is relief from all sense of responsibility. It may feel like a relief for a short time, but then we start to feel restless, unfulfilled, and bored with life. We get a certain sense of peace that we are avoiding failure, disappointment, and maybe even catastrophe. But these happy schmucks all around me, the ones with all the friends, are always running toward the next challenge.

Do these excuses sound familiar?
- *I don't have enough time*
- *I don't have enough money*
- *If I fail, I will feel so embarrassed*
- *It's probably not as great of an idea as I think*
- *I have a family to take care of*
- *If I had started when I were younger*
- *I just don't know enough about it*
- *It would require so much work*
- *I'll probably just lose interest anyway*

These are the words of someone who has mastered the art of pretending to value an average, comfortable life. A therapist once asked me what my goals and dreams were. I sat there with a completely blank look and nothing to say.

I seriously had not thought about that question in years, and I didn't know the answer. When I told her I couldn't think of anything, she asked me to try to think of just one. Still, nothing. I had achieved all my goals, I told her. I had a college degree, a smart and healthy son, a noble career, and good health. What else was I supposed to be aiming for?

I left her office that day realizing that one of two things must be true. Either I had achieved all of my goals and dreams at the age of 38 and have possibly sentenced myself to another 40+ years of boredom, or I have yet to discover an unrealized dream or some goal that will bring me a deeper sense of fulfillment. The latter ended up being true, but of course I had to go through some really crappy stuff before I understood what was happening.

I still haven't mastered the art of the badass, but I knew the moment I discovered my passion that I had discovered the energy to pursue it. This all happened during one of the biggest upturns in my life. That seems pretty badass to me.

I hope this book helps you see that your crappy stuff can propel you into finding your passion too.

As Long as You Never Give Up, a Challenge Never Becomes a Struggle

I had spent years looking at life as a series of struggles to avoid instead of a series of challenges to overcome. Once I learned to embrace that life is a process and not a destination, I began to see that my life could go in any direction I choose. My worst critic has been myself all along. I had settled for where I had arrived because it seemed like that was what I wanted: enough money to live comfortably, no major problems for myself or my loved ones, and a dog who is happy to see me when I come home.

The thought was nagging me that if I had already achieved my goals in life, I should have every right to hold my head up high in any setting. I should be carrying myself with a sense of confidence that can't be shaken. Instead, looking back, I was still reading all kinds of books on self-confidence, self-esteem, and self-improvement. If I had already achieved my goals, what was I trying to improve?

I realized that I wasn't trying to improve anything. I was trapped in a cocoon of safety and comfort. In other words, I was too afraid of losing any of my comforts to take any significant risks. I was addicted to the comforts of being average. After enough time had passed with this attitude, I forgot how to use my ability to see what *could* be. It doesn't have to be about money, or fame, or a sports career. It can be something as simple as saving for that trip you have always wanted to take, buying that luxury car you always said would strap you financially, or sitting down to write that book you've always talked about.

Dreams and goals can change, too. Just make sure you don't forget to have at least one dream in sight at all times. This, just so you know, is one of the character traits of those people that have their priorities in order. They know what they want, their dreams, and they judge everything they do by a simple litmus test. They ask themselves, *"Does this choice promote my goals?"* And if the answer is *yes*, they very well might jump in. They are not afraid of risk. It might seem risky or foolish, but badasses know that there will be all kinds of bumps and pitfalls. The point was never to avoid challenges, but to achieve a personally-meaningful goal regardless of them.

Those who walk around with no idea what their purpose is on earth probably make their decisions based on a different litmus test. They ask themselves, *"Is there a risk I might experience pain or disappointment?"* The irony is that by following this guideline for every decision, we will disappoint ourselves by default, and the pain of not having acted on our deepest values and dreams is worse than a little embarrassment after an unsuccessful attempt.

Let me clarify that any goal or dream is worthy of your effort. Raising a child is a very noble task, and most parents find great fulfillment in raising their children the very best they know how. Being a good parent becomes a lifestyle for some people, and I think that illustrates perfectly how we much treat every dream and goal. Think of the sacrifices parents make for their children. They might quit smoking, quit drinking, start looking for a better job, move to a nicer neighborhood, take the child to the doctor even when it might be nothing, and there's the future time and money investments that really start adding up long before they turn 18. Even then, the social obligations and financial rescues may keep coming. Do you give so much of yourself because you feel like you have to? The happiest parents like being able to help their children, while skillfully guiding them toward the best next step. When, one day, they no longer require our financial help, we hope they will never lose that most important connection, the bond that was the real investment all along.

This is a dream and a goal worth spending your life on, but unless your parent-child obligation requires daily care because of their condition, there is plenty of room in your life for other meaningful things. In fact, you could consider it an important aspect of parenting: demonstrating for your child (or children) that even later in life, when they have children of their own, they can still find fulfillment in setting goals and pursuing dreams. The lesson you teach by the example you set will impact your child's peace of mind throughout their entire life.

<u>Struggle</u> is a weight; <u>challenge</u> is an opportunity.

Struggle says, "I can't wait for this to be done." Challenge says, "I can't wait to see where this goes." Struggle says, "How can I get out?" but challenge says, "How can I excel?"

Struggling is resisting and complaining about what life is giving you, and it will exhaust you.

When you are in a challenge, you get all that latent competitive energy. The time flies like it does any time you're playing any other game that YOU are in. This will exhaust you sometimes too, but in a way that comes with a sense of accomplishment and deep inner-satisfaction.

Think about something important to you that you're working on improving: a relationship, a project, a goal. Now think about the energy around that thing. Are you in a struggle or are you in a challenge? Since you're going to come out of it exhausted either way, you might as well have fun.

Turning Humiliation into a Rebirth

When I stopped drinking alcohol, I was not trying to make anyone proud. I knew that I had this horrible tendency to make bad decisions when I drank alcohol, and it was seriously affecting my physical health as well. I could not continue living that way, so I sought help. Through lessons in humility, honesty, trust, and faith, I went from a daily drinker to a frequent designated driver. It wasn't easy, but somehow I scraped together enough self-love to choose life over my favorite numbing agent.

Honestly, it was for two reasons that I stopped drinking. Reason #1: The embarrassing situations I caused in my life would never be forgivable (my thinking at the time) if I didn't show a distinct change in my life's direction. Reason #2: Jeopardizing my role in my son's life was a cost I was not willing to pay. From the time he was in his mother's belly, I made a sacred promise to him and to myself that I would always be there for him. Drinking every day had become a habit that was now in direct opposition to my values and was definitely not helping me achieve my goal of being there for my son. Of course, none of this became obvious to me until later. . (Please know that I do not have anything against drinking alcohol, as long as you're not using it to constantly cover issues that would be better dealt with). I stopped drinking because I had humiliated myself and trashed a friend's house. She was paying me to housesit while she and her family were out of town. It happened to be at about the same time that I got a huge refill on my Xanax and found a bottle of wine that my ex and I bought together. In a symbolic gesture, I drank the whole bottle in one evening, along with a regular dose of my tranquilizers every five or six hours. I wasn't trying to kill myself, but it sure would have seemed like it to any observer.

While on this strange bender, I decided to get on Facebook and say a bunch of things to my family that I would never say sober. In fact, some of the things I said were not even true, but I guess I thought they were at the time. I ranted against my mother, publicly criticizing her parenting, I insulted other family members, all of whom I love dearly, and mostly over issues that were years old and very exaggerated in my head. I could not re-gain my self-respect unless I demonstrated a radical reversal of trajectory.

My motives for getting sober were selfish at the time, but it wasn't long before I realized how much my change in behavior was making a huge positive difference in the lives of those I cared about most. A year after I stopped drinking, my mother decided she had enough of her dependency on pain pills. My ex-wife, empowered by my admission of being an alcoholic, created life-changing friendships among women who relate with her. My son told me, a few years later, that he was proud of me for giving up alcohol. Without knowing it, I was teaching him a lesson that could very easily save his life. Serious issues with alcohol affected my own father, his father, and my mother's father. My son was watching me choose to stop drinking, do the necessary work, and although I am by no means perfect, he treats that choice I made as if I won some world championship.

The Tao Te Ching, verse 3, says:
When a leader shows self-discipline,
there is peace in the kingdom.

I wanted relief and forgiveness. My goal was to stop drinking and win back the respect I thought I had lost. That was my goal. It sounds like I was mostly thinking about my pride at the time, and you'd be right. Thankfully, however, it would end up being the best thing I could have done for not just myself, but everyone I love. By setting my sights on new higher expectations, everyone I love benefitted in amazing ways. Can you tell me that my selfish reasons for quitting alcohol didn't have a hundred unselfish effects? That might be true, but a badass wouldn't even analyze it that much. My inner badass says it's a waste of time questioning my motivation for quitting alcohol. It was an excellent decision and I know it.

I Get By with a Little Help

A real badass doesn't take sole credit for anything. The truth is nobody on earth deserves sole credit for anything they've accomplished. If you can't thank anyone for helping you or giving you what it takes to be a badass, then you will probably end up a smart ass, or a dumb ass, instead of a badass. Badasses know that they would be nowhere without the people who believe in them, whether it's a parent or a Sunday school teacher.

Here are some examples of people we could thank for making us who we are today:

- Our parents, whether by good example or bad, usually played a big role in showing us the difference between a victor and a victim

- Who was around when you were growing up? We can sometimes only remember faces, but we have been influenced by enough people to fill a large auditorium. From the cool kid we wanted to hang out with down the block, to the stranger who told us that we had a lot of talent. It takes a village of badasses to raise a badass.

- Your school teachers, while often overlooked as simply underpaid public servants, have a huge role in shaping the average person. I learned much more about living life from school than I did about how to type in MLA Format. My teachers, by example only, helped me understand the kind of person I wanted to be. That 10th-grade United States history teacher who just sat there doing nothing while he assigned you to read a chapter over 30 pages long—he was one of the teachers who taught me what kind of person I don't want to be. There were so many that set good examples, though. The teachers who cared taught me that there is a lot of value in being able to articulate what I want to say in the most effective and efficient way. I want to explain things to other people in a way that makes them smile, or better yet, in a way that makes them appreciate the subject on a deeper level. My teachers all helped me learn how to do that.

- Your badass aunt, father, brother, cousin, mother, grandfather, grandmother, uncle, or even your badass child might deserve a heartfelt thank-you for helping to make you the badass you are today. Keep the list going and you'll always find yourself adding to it. I cannot name every person in my life who has taught me how to use my badass powers, because I can't think of anyone who hasn't taught me by their example. Everyone has something to teach us, and if we are in tune with this aspect of human relationships, we will start to understand why everyone deserves to feel comfortable expressing a badass attitude. We are all badasses in our own way.

When I started reading self-help books about the law of attraction, I was looking everywhere for the part where they explain that a generous spirit and a respect for other people is the single most effective way to maximize the money you are trying to attract.

Holiday Survival Guide

<u>**Here are the most critical points to remember if you get the Holiday Blues:**</u>

Determine ahead of time how much you can afford to spend on gifts. Stick to your budget, and make no excuses.
Remember: There is no such thing as a perfect Christmas. The ideal holiday, as portrayed in movies and sometimes occupy our childhood memories, are not accurate. This Christmas will be as perfect as you have determined to view it.
Enjoy the little things. Each moment has something that is worth smiling about. You just have to get out of your own head long enough to see it.
Donating your time to help the less fortunate is a great way to boost your joy during the holiday season. Some people make it clear that they will be giving all of their time and money to a local soup kitchen this Christmas. You'd be surprised how big you will make others smile.
Gratitude list: Make a special holiday edition of your gratitude list. There's no better time to be thankful for what we already have than during the holidays.
If someone suggests an adventure or activity, say yes!
If you enjoy church, get involved during the holidays.
Re-write the holidays. If you could make Christmas into anything you wanted, how would you re-invent the whole holiday? Write it down in your journal.
You are not the only one who gets the holiday blues. If your depression gets serious, or you are considering any self-harm, please seek out a professional. This is a common problem, and talking to a professional about it often snaps us out of it quickly. There is nothing to be embarrassed about.

Your Dreams Are Waiting for You to Remember Them

You may not be able to identify your dreams right now, but you do have them. If you have tried and tried to figure out what your dreams are and still draw a blank, it's time to talk to our parents or a trusted relative. What did you enjoy doing as a child? What goals did you have? And as you ask them these questions, remember what it felt like back then and how easily you connected a goal with the promise of future peace of mind. Everything that has clouded your memory between then and now has been a symptom of belonging in the illusion of time. <u>As the "Tao of the River" says, time is only an illusion; there has only been THE NOW all along.</u> If you can't think of a dream worth pursuing, it's time to ask your inner child. He or she is there, don't worry, you're just going to have to let some memories take you back there. I guess it's time to pull up some old photos or call an old friend.

<u>Try this mental exercise to get your self-worth in perspective</u>:

Imagine there is someone who sits beside you on the bus every day who tells you that you are too much of a coward to really pursue your dreams. Now imagine that same person saying those same words to a child who sits next to him on a bus. Now imagine anyone accusing Oprah Winfrey, Caitlyn Jenner, Michael Jordan, or Bill Gates of being a coward. Which person among those mentioned above deserves being called weak? You?

How to Quiet Your Mind the First Time, Every Time

There is a proven method for quieting these voices. I call it The Golden Reminder. It is a very fast practice that can be done any time of the day, as often during the day as needed, and once the brain's programming is rewired properly, you will notice that the effects of The Golden Reminder start to last longer and longer. Some people may need to meditate on The Golden Reminder several times daily at first. I find it especially helpful to repeat it before beginning a book, a painting, or a nap.

Some people might call it worrying. Other words for the aimless, usually negative, always distracting, self-talk that many of us deal with. I used to believe that I needed to have to sleep with the television on in order to fall asleep and stay asleep. While this was definitely a step above vodka with a beer chaser, it was still a temporary solution to a chronic problem. Why must I end the day with an exhausted brain when it wasn't even a very bad day?

So, when you notice the inner dialog starting to become a distraction, repeat the following sentences exactly and let each one sink all the way in before moving to the next one. It should not take longer than two minutes, and might be particularly useful in all kinds of situations.

The Golden Reminder

1. Past thoughts are not useful to me right now.
2. Thoughts of the future are imaginary movies that need to be turned off right now.
3. I will love myself enough to be myself, including my good qualities and my vulnerabilities.
4. I will trust in life enough to let it play out the way it is supposed to.
5. I consciously decide to direct my mind to quietly accept the Now.
6. The Now that requires my full attention will not allow useless self-talk to distract me.

You can use this meditation before giving a speech, before calling the electric company to set up payment arrangements, before reading a book, before bed, before prayer. In some ways, it can act as a pre-meditation meditation. If you want to conquer your bad mood and turn it into a badass attitude, you might have to practice The Golden Reminder often at first. If you are the type, like me, who is constantly talking himself or herself into something or out of something, you'll need to keep repeating the Golden Reminder every day, especially before picking this book back up again.

What Makes Someone Insecure

It had never occurred to me to research the subject of insecurity because I always labeled myself as insecure. I thought I knew the subject first-hand. It turns out that while that is true, I can see that I am not the only one. These are common human characteristics, but they can reveal an insecurity if you look carefully:

- People who are insecure are always bringing up their accomplishments. There is an unconscious fear that if they are too quiet, it will be assumed they are not smart. This may appear as bragging, but it is a cry for external validation. This can be a hard habit to break.

- Insecure people tend to use the act of pointing out flaws wherever they notice them as a conversation starter. I catch myself doing this, and I make a conscious effort to find something good to mention instead.

- Insecure people seem generally unhappy with the way things are right now. There may be an infinite mental list of ways they wish things were different. This coping mechanism helps to deflect from unresolved inner pain, shame, worry, or whatever is causing their insecurity.

- Insecure people, if you don't set clear healthy boundaries, will try to make you feel insecure too. Usually this is unconscious, and can often come with good intentions. ("I'm just trying to keep her head out of the clouds--she could never get a guy like him.") While this seems cruel as an outsider, many people value insecurity and will redefine it as "being realistic." Remind them that there's enough realism in the real world to kill every dream ever dreamt, and the precious few that show signs of life should be tenderly nourished.

- A negative self-image is commonly correlated with insecurity. Someone who thinks their nose is too big will literally find it difficult to hold their head up high after years of trying to keep their face in the shadows. I grew up with crooked teeth and to this day I almost never smile for a photo with an open mouth. The good news is that this part of an insecure personality is easily treatable, without cosmetic surgery.

- One dead giveaway for identifying an insecure person is to look deeper into what they are criticizing. If you notice that they are unknowingly criticizing things in others that are especially sensitive issues for them. For example, if a person feels like the way they draw makes them look stupid, they might be prone to stop attempting any more drawing of their own and since the self-criticism hurts, they might find comfort in criticizing your drawing.

- Insecure people are not good candidates for conversion into a life of positivity and dream-building. The best way to win them over is by showing them instead of explaining it. If it sounds like a plan, they will start to crouch like a lioness, ready to pounce on your idea until they find the jugular. For your own survival, do not explain your goals and dreams to insecure people, ever. Tell them all about it after you make it a reality, but don't expect them to buy into your dream at all if you're still in the planning stages. They might not mean to be cruel, but they will find a certain satisfaction in watching the hope drain from your eyes. Don't hang out with people like that too much.

- On a serious note, remember that many, if not most, insecure personalities have past issues that they have been dealing with for a long time. Insecurity may be the result of past abuse, whether physical, emotional, sexual, or verbal. This means that they may have a long journey before they can be transformed by forgiveness and acceptance. This is a journey they will need to complete at their own pace. Do not offer unsolicited advice. Their story is not our story, and a certain level of empathy and usage of the hands-off approach will be required if you are to learn the ways of a master badass.

No Victims, Just Quiet Heros and Badass Painters

Everybody deals with insecurity on some level. I have consciously tried to keep my criticisms low-key, implementing my plans and goals without much fanfare. This helps me feel like the pressure is off because the spotlight is not on me. I love sharing noteworthy accomplishments with my close friends but I don't discuss my accomplishments with very many others. The only time it is appropriate to share your accomplishments is if it is very relevant or if the other person asks you about it. Have I accomplished anything in my life worth mentioning? Of course I have! Jesus said it best when he explained that if you do something for the recognition, you will get your reward. If you get your thrill from telling others about your accomplishments, then once they've heard you brag about it, your payoff is over. Jesus was referring to charitable giving, but I think it applies to much more.

I will now share with you my favorite secret about humility. The less you brag, the more they will assume you have, or the smarter they will assume you are. Quiet people, some might describe them as having a stoic stance, are nearly always assumed to be cleverly observing everything, guarding countless secrets of the universe, and even if they spoke up, I might look stupid if it goes over my head.

The truth is usually the opposite. I must have a contemplative resting face because often I am assumed to be lost in complex thought, when actually I am engaging in some sort of typical mundane fantasy and counting the minutes until I can be somewhere else. In summary, the less you say, the more they will assume you know.

This is the first principle, and this will start our list of principles and suggestions for turning a bad mood into a badass attitude. Remember, these are principles, not commandments. I cannot promise that if you obey a certain list of instructions you can achieve self-confidence. It cannot be put into a universal equation and more than learning to ride a bike can be learned by listening to instructions. You need to review these principles every day. Internalize them, practice them, rehearse them, journal about them, and believe that I am telling you the truth. If you can integrate the following principles into your daily life, you will notice a serious change in your attitude toward life. (From now on, think victor, not victim.)

- The less you say in a group, the smarter you are assumed to be. If you want to keep them thinking that forever, then only chime in when a topic is being discussed that you know enough to discuss. Opinions do not count, and opinions are not equated with intelligence in the real world. In fact, a lot has been said about overly-opinionated people, none of it is good.
- Reschedule your week to include more time around people who make you feel accepted for who you are. Friends that encourage you to follow your dreams are golden, spend more time with them, and maybe encourage them a little more now that you realize how precious they have been all this time.
- Every day is spa day. People with high self-love will take their time to transform their grooming habits into a series of luxurious daily rituals. If you treat your morning bathroom routines like a visit to the spa, you will start the day off so right. If you battle regularly with bad hair days, it's time to ask the lady who cuts your hair for advice. Ask if she has any style suggestions for your body shape

and hair type, and ask her to jot down on paper what you should do every morning to achieve that same look. Then leave her twice your normal tip. That's what a badass would do.

    a. I am more concerned about getting everything cleaned and presentable in a timely fashion when it comes to morning bathroom routine. I have a simple step-by-step mental order of operations for bathing, grooming, and dressing, and the end result emerging from the bathroom looks exactly like the guy who just finished getting ready yesterday. Since my routine is so simple, I make a big deal out of the music I listen to while taking my morning shower. For me, a few uplifting songs while making the whole bathroom smell like shampoo is enough to start me off on the right foot. Whatever it takes to make grooming fun. If you are a badass, you demand to look and smell your best, so it is critical to enjoy the time you spend designing your look for the day. (Think about how much those people love their dogs who brush them as an idle activity. Or, maybe less weird, think of someone painstakingly polishing their brand new car. This is how you treat the things you care about. Start applying this principle to yourself)

- While we're on the subject of good looks, take full advantage of a good hair day, or a day when you just feel great being alive, and have a good friend (preferably someone who has decent selfie skills) to take your picture. Make it look unplanned if possible, but make sure your friend knows you're going for the most flattering pose for a profile picture. Now you have just turned that good hair day into a good hair year. Once you have a great profile pic, stick with it. Changing it too often makes you seem vain anyway.

- Explore untried talents. **Ever pick up a paintbrush?** Canvases are not expensive, and acrylic paints are a fun and easy way to express yourself and create beautiful things to look at. For the first 39 years of my life, I found coloring, drawing, and painting about as fun as the average person. My downfall came when I started comparing my works of art to the masters. What a cruel form of self-sabotage. I have two tips for feeling like a great painter after just one attempt.

    Step One: Have a minimum of **three** colors (or various shades of the same color) on your pallet at a time. Let them mix and see how the blending colors inspire you to create color blends on the canvas. Don't try to create a Mona Lisa on the first day. There's already enough Mona Lisas anyway. Just have fun with shapes and blending colors. Never put your brush to the canvas without at least two distinct colors on the brush. Blending is the key to disguising mistakes. (You can even use my own personal trick: If I mess up badly on a part of a painting, I will let the universe guide my hand as to how to cover it up. Once I painted a big scene with a field, a barn, a horse, a farmer, and a house. I didn't know when to stop with the house I guess, because I was very happy with the whole painting, but the house just didn't seem to feel right. That's when I got the brilliant idea to paint the house as if it were on fire. I had not yet attempted to paint flames, let alone a whole house aflame, but I sure had fun practicing on the house I messed up.)

    Step Two: If you absolutely must compare your art with another artist's work, compare your paintings to those of Jackson Pollock.

This was one of my first paintings.
I was channeling my inner-Jackson Pollock.
I don't care what anyone says, there is no right or wrong in art.

Now you can walk with the confidence of an artist who has created a work of art, and since beauty is in the eye of the beholder, you are free to pick which of your own paintings are your favorite and consider it a masterpiece in your own home. Remember, though, do not brag about how great your first series of paintings are, just wait for someone to come inside your house and ask you if that's really your signature at the bottom.

This principle works for any potential hobby and also for any new adventure you will indulge in. Badasses love adventure. The adventurous spirit does not come naturally to me. I get very irritated by change and I catch myself being terribly critical of everything I do. That kind of habitual negativity eventually led me to a sort of creative paralysis. For me, the key to overcoming the fear of looking like an idiot was so simple, I just had to do it once, and decide for myself if I enjoyed it. I tried hiking, it was a good activity, until I got left in the dust by my hiking partner who was ten years younger than me. I tried camping, and even though it was not even remotely as cool as camping-enthusiasts make it sound, I also didn't hate it, and since I gave it an honest attempt with an open mind, I can now say I do not hate camping, but I would rather not. I tried sculpting, and made one sculpture that resembles an Easter Island head with warrior paint. I didn't love the process, so I crossed that off my list too. Painting and sketching art seemed to stick the longest. Interestingly, I have no remarkable talent for either, but since I am enjoying the process, the quality of my art is evolving into something I can call a hobby. Not everyone would find my art appealing, but I do, and my son does, and I don't really need to waste any more time worrying about who likes it when I could spend that same time creating a new one.

Do not be too critical of yourself!
About anything!

"The fact that we live at the bottom of a deep gravity well, on the surface of a gas covered planet going around a nuclear fireball 90 million miles away and think this to be normal is obviously some indication of how skewed our perspective tends to be."

— Douglas Adams, *The Salmon of Doubt: Hitchhiking the Galaxy One Last Time*

Don't Criticize Yourself, Ever! (And Other Secrets of the Badass)

- Badasses are very generous, even when it requires an occasional sacrifice. I'm not talking about the Salvation Army bell-ringers (although I see no harm in giving them my spare change at least once every Christmas season), but actual generosity. Maybe you have a little extra money, and a coworker's car needs a new radiator. Sneak them a little cash anonymously, and maybe add a note that you hope this money helps pay for their new radiator. Whether they figure out it was you or not, or even if you just can't keep it a secret, do it out of kindness and don't tell anyone else. And for goodness sake, never call it a loan. Stop loaning people money. If you have it to loan, you have it to give. When you do not expect to be repaid, you will be surprised how many people will repay you with interest, and even if they don't, the rewards that will come from a truly selfless act will be priceless. You won't know what it feels like until you do it.

> "The river gives without getting. For this reason it will never stop flowing."
> –The Tao of the River v. 13

- Know what you value most. Before you go starting vision boards, you need to start a list of things that matter most to you in life. Keep adding to the list as you think of more to add. Edit, revise, and augment your list as needed. After some days have passed, if you have worked on your list, you will have created an invaluable document. Frame it. Refer to this list for inspiration, encouragement, and for direction in making decisions.

  > This is not a test. Your list doesn't have to be a list of people you love, followed by humble requests for this or that if there's enough for you to have some too. Be real and raw about your list—nobody needs to see it but you. If you love meeting up with your secret lover more than anything in the world, add it to your list (might want to use a secret code for that one). If you love skinny dipping in the pool at night after everyone is fast asleep, write that down too (in code also). You're not filling out a dating profile questionnaire, so be honest with yourself. Set all preconceived judgments aside and ask yourself sincerely, what really matters most to you?

- Become knowledgeable about your job, no matter how much you are ready to quit. Study the company, the brand, do your assigned tasks with care to detail, do more than is required to keep your workplace clean and tidy, show up early and leave late, and treat every coworker with respect. You will find that before long, you will either begin to enjoy your job on a new level, or you will see signs of new opportunities ahead. If your job is already a professional career for which you are trained, make efforts to expand your expertise in unconventional ways. Of course you could take that class you have been meaning to sign up for and that is required to maintain your certification, but if you want to be a badass, you'll go beyond that. Find someone in your community who is a consummate professional with a great reputation and shadow them. Watch videos online that will give you new insight or that will be a refresher.

- While you are in the learning mode, I would like to suggest something that you are possibly going to roll your eyes at. You may say no way, but please consider looking into it before you say never. I would suggest that you enroll in some sort of class at your local college. I honestly believe it could transform your life. You may think you hate school, and you will hate taking a class, but I promise it is potentially a huge adventure waiting for you to enroll, right there in your own town.

I'm not suggesting a math class, or microbiology, unless you love those topics. It is crucial that you choose a subject that you already have a genuine curiosity about. Painting, basket-weaving, Native American culture, Eastern religions, an introduction to a foreign language, creative writing, public speaking, sculpting, interior design, you name it. Get online now to see what kind of classes offered by your nearest college might possibly be interesting to you. Get prices. If you do end up in an appointment with a registration counselor, make sure they understand you are only interested in taking a fun easy course for no credit, as a way to keep your mind sharp. All I ask is that you seriously investigate what you'd need to do to take a college class for enrichment purposes (might be much cheaper than taking the same class for credit you'll never use). You will thank me later.

- Every time you catch yourself making a list of problems you have to deal with, make a list of solutions.

"We are all leaders if even for ourselves
Do not embrace a problem
Until you reframe it as an opportunity"
--The Tao of the River, verse 13

The Wrong Way to Write a To-Do List:

___ Fix leaky roof
___ Wash clothes after work
___ Ask for Friday off
___ Buy new school shirt for Jenny

The Right Way to Write a To-Do List:

- Submit day-off request before clocking out
- Paperclip a reminder on time card
- Stop by hardware store on the way home
- Explain problem to helpful hardware man
- Explain how much you can afford
- Look over the products he recommends
- Purchase best affordable roof repair stuff
- Call Uncle Fred for advice on repairing a roof
- Start load of clothes before sitting down
- Add five new things to my gratitude journal
- Watch an episode of my favorite show (just one)
- Put laundry in the dryer
- Read *Turn Your Bad Mood into a Badass Attitude*

- When Jenny gets home from school, fold the laundry with her while planning a shopping trip to buy her a new school shirt.
- While we're out, take Jenny to get an ice cream at her favorite place. While we're enjoying the ice cream, listen to every word she says and before you leave the ice cream place, take a serious moment to tell her one specific reason she is such a remarkable daughter.

- Get your body moving! I know I said I didn't love hiking, but that was because the person I was hiking with was more interested in the forest than the company I was providing. Also, I was unaware of my limitations, so I foolishly agreed to a trail with a hellish incline. But just because I didn't love hiking doesn't mean I am exempt from the principle of exercising.

    You do not have to run, lift weights, attempt a push up, or blow out your knee doing burpees. You can get a tremendous benefit from walking around the block a few times a week. If the weather isn't cooperating, you can borrow my trick. I get all of my exercise from dancing around my house to loud music or making sure I get my heart rate up at least once per day somehow.

- Give up television. I used to scoff at this suggestion because it felt like I would be sentencing myself to a life of boredom, but quite the contrary. Television kept me very distracted while I mastered the art of sloth. Television should be treated like any technological tool, and there is time enough each day to catch up on your soap, catch the headlines, or glance at the score of the game every once in a while. However, I can do all of this on my laptop also, and I am not glued to my sofa while I absorb 90% advertisement and 10% hype. If you can keep your TV off for more than 50% of your waking hours at home, you will start to notice all of the other things that need to be done, or that you have been wanting to do.

    If you can manage to turn your television off for 48 hours straight, you'll realize how bored you have been this whole time. You've been too distracted to notice, but you have been bored out of your mind for as long as television has seemed entertaining to you. Television is not designed to be helpful or entertaining. The programming chosen by most stations is designed to keep you watching. Keep you hanging. Keep you from changing the channel. It's a product that promises entertainment, and often captures our attention with a well-written show, but the vast majority of the content on all of television is advertising and programming filler. Stop wasting precious minutes of life staring at a TV screen.

- In another section of your gratitude journal (you know the journal where you need to be updating your gratitude list daily), you will need to also start an ongoing list of personal accomplishments, no matter how small. More will come to mind as time passes, so treat this list like a living document, adding to it regularly as we remember past accomplishments and earn new ones.

    Do you remember how good it felt as a kid to get a genuine pat on the back, or a sincere, "Good job!"? That doesn't stop just because you grow up, it just becomes your responsibility to pat yourself on the back, and mean it. Unfortunately, not enough people figure this out before they've spent years of feeling like their accomplishments have never been noteworthy. On the contrary, everything you have accomplished is another reason that you deserve to feel like a badass, but if you're waiting for someone else to notice how well your efforts are turning out, you might be waiting forever. No, sadly, the incentives for reaching goals and doing a great job are for you to set, so make it worthwhile. If you cheat,

no one but you will know, but also no one will be missing out except you. Reward yourself, work hard for the reward, and since you will become your favorite boss ever, make sure you are your new boss' favorite employee.
When you accomplish something, you deserve to feel good about it, just like everyone should. You know what took a lot of effort and what project was easy. Sometimes it's the thing that took the most effort, and we are most proud of, that gets the fewest compliments. Start valuing your accomplishments more than other people's opinions.

- I know this assignment is especially difficult for certain depressive-types (like me), so make sure you add to your accomplishments that you are taking your mental health seriously and are willing to do the work required in order to feel like the badass you are.

**"Restrain yourself and you will be free from restraint.
It is because the river flooded that the first dam was built."
--The Tao of The River, verse 8**

The Woods Are Lovely, Dark, and Deep (But I Have Pages to Write Before I Sleep)

<u>Journaling</u>

For the sake of simplicity, let's just get one blank journal. It can be an old notebook with half the pages still blank, or you can go to the store and buy a fancy one. I always check to make sure it is either college ruled or completely blank. You might not feel this way, but I have a strong bias against wide ruled paper. I used to exclusively buy college ruled until I started trying all kinds of art media. I stumbled on some really nice blank sketchbooks 9"x6" for less than a dollar each, so I bought all they had, I think about 7 or 8 blank sketchbooks, brought them home, and as soon as I could I tried using one as a journal. No lines! Who would have thought? I do end up writing too big probably, but because of the freedom to take notes in creatively-organized ways has made jotting down my ideas and lists a lot more expressive.

If you want a plain spiral notebook, that will work. There are blank journals at the dollar store that look expensive, there are expensive-style notebooks at a discount at stores like Ross. There are some really fancy ones at the big retailers, but you may pay a fancy price for a bunch of blank pages. Then again, these are your words and your thoughts, so maybe that should be the most valuable book in the house.

Once you have your journal, designate a place to keep it where it will not fall into nosey hands. Don't forget to choose a pen that feels comfortable while writing, you want this to be a pleasant experience. Maybe light a candle, some incense, soft piano music, and fold your feet up under you on the big comfy chair you bought just to use for reading that you rarely use.

Your journal with evolve as we continue this process, so just pay attention to the journal alerts like the one below. This will help you to not miss a single journal instruction.

Journal Update

Every time you see this box, look for the journal instructions. Remember, your journal is a crucial component to becoming a genuine badass.

Before your begin writing in your journal, think of it as a canvas for your brain words. It doesn't have to make sense to anyone but you. It is like an external hard drive that is only compatible with your laptop. If something comes to mind, write it down, no matter how silly it seems, you can always tear it out later, if you decide you feel too silly, but just writing it down relieves so much pressure from your working memory and emotional memory, your brain will be thanking you.

We are going to title it "Gratitude Journal". Leave it at that, with your first name and last initial on the inside cover. The title is clearly indicative of someone's private writing, but the name "Gratitude Journal" is boring enough to keep them out of it.

Not ironically, our first writing challenge is to think of ten things we are grateful for right now in our lives. I'll start:

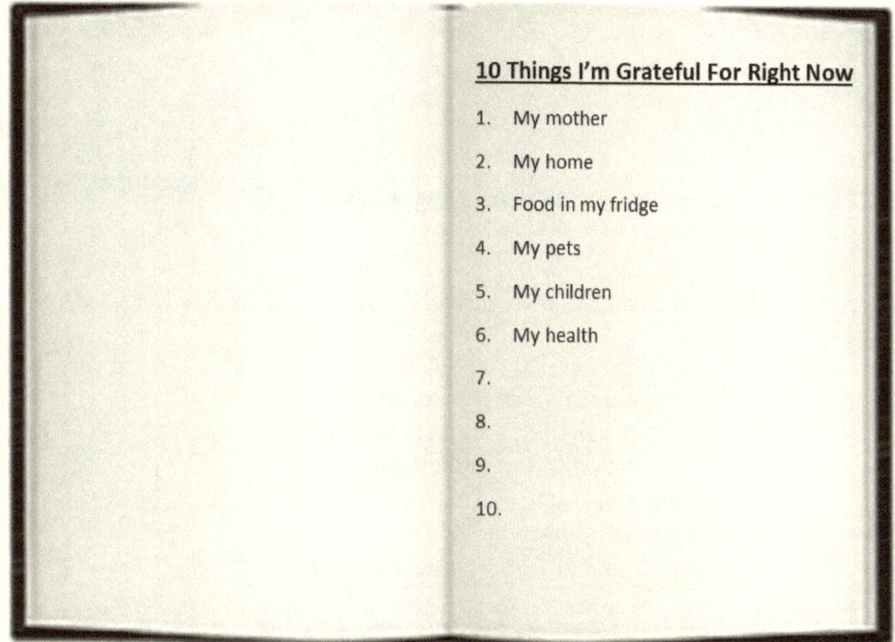

Keep it simple. If this becomes a laborious exercise, you will dread future entries, so try to have fun with it. If you are so inclined, you can decorate your books with doodles that remind you of the list items or maybe even some other things that just make you happy. As an example, I like seahorses, so I might decorate the opposite page with a seahorse doodle. You can get as creative as you want, as long as you end up with a list of ten things you are grateful for.

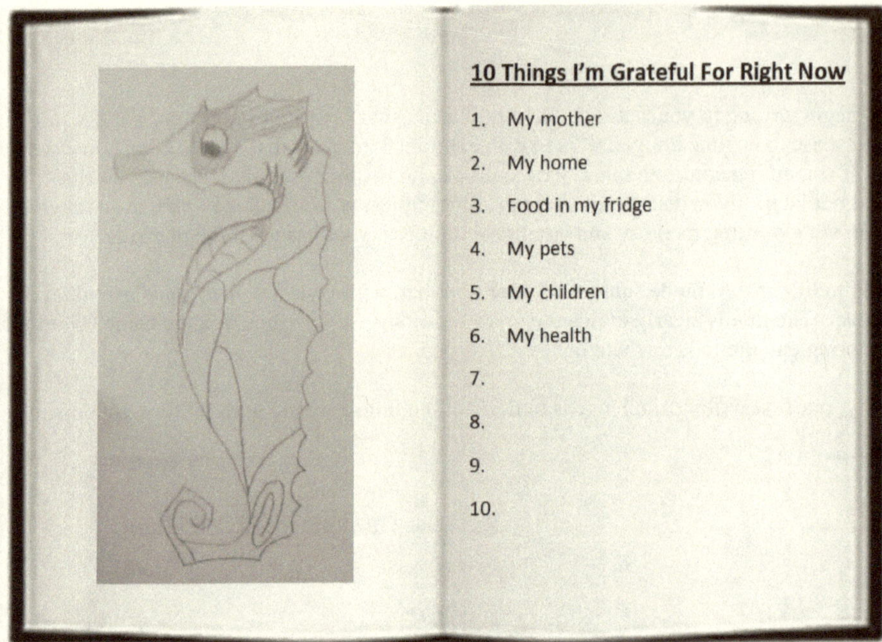

If you are having trouble thinking of things to be grateful for, you can use the following idea list to jog your memory:

Good health (yours and others)
Spouse, children, parents, other loved ones
Home, shelter, comforts of living
Food, drinkable water
Income, assets of financial security
Opportunities you have or have had
Accomplishments (yours and others)

If it doesn't come easily at first, it doesn't mean that you are an ungrateful brat, it just sometimes takes a little mind exercising before your brain gets used to seeing the world through a lens of gratitude. It will get much easier, and even a little fun. Makes for a great way to end the day before you drift away into dreamland.

Ok, your list of ten things, you did that right? Don't forget to go back and make a list of the badasses in your life that you admire. Be specific. What exactly makes them a badass in your eyes?
Now that the writing assignments are complete, let us proceed with transforming our bad mood into a much-more-fun badass attitude. We have all pretended to be a badass at one time or another. When I was a kid, I remember thinking that the key in being a badass was to make any emotion as subtle as possible, quietly watch the other people react around you, while you maintain a poker face, state your objective simply, and flash your shiny pistol as if you are keeping it a secret from everyone

except the bad guy. I guess my idea of a badass is a Clint Eastwood type that commands total respect from the entire room.

I have had many opportunities to talk to a captive group of people, sometimes I was not very well-prepared, other times I had everyone's attention, and a few times I made a whole room laugh. That felt pretty badass. I noticed a pattern, too. The more prepared I was, the calmer I was, and it was when I delivered well-rehearsed lines with confidence that I knocked it out of the park every time.

At the age of about 18 or 19, I had the opportunity to be the speaker during morning chapel where I was attending college. I prepared well, rehearsed it all in front of an audience of trusted critics, and after a few finishing touches, I felt like I could have given that speech to Congress. The day came, I prayed and meditated, trusted my preparation, and with limited shaking I delivered my ten-minute sermon to the entire student body. I don't remember being on stage that day because I have a tendency to black out whenever I am speaking in front of crowds. Still, I learned that I cannot expect self-confidence unless I also invest my time and hard work into developing successful habits. Margaret Thatcher once said, "I do not know anyone who has gotten to the top without hard work. That is the recipe. It will not always get you to the top, but should get you pretty near."
My point was not to brag about how prepared I was that one day. Follow my logic:
     i.   Dirty-Harry-style confidence is badass.
    ii.   Being well-prepared makes me feel confident even when I'm taking risks.
   iii.   If I approach life like I did my chapel talk, I will not worry so much about my problems.
   iv.   If I also put real effort into changing my attitude, by doing the gratitude journal, I will be arrive in BadassLand any time now.

Be a Badass (Not a Punk Ass, Jackass, Pain-in-the-Ass,Smart Ass, Lazy Ass, Ass-Kisser or Dumb Ass)

(Sometimes a hard-ass is appropriate, and it's okay to kick ass at something, but please don't be an a**hole)

What Makes Someone a Badass?

Being a badass, like any other attitude, is not always immediately noticeable. Real badasses always float to the top of the lake, but the science is fuzzy for identifying a badass by a specifc set of characteristics. Here are some very common traits that are quite likely indicative of some badassery:

- They are fiercely loyal lovers and friends. Loyal, as in they will not tell your secrets to the other person they're having an affair with. They are definitely not immune to temptations of the flesh.

- They carry themselves with humility, never ashamed to learn something new that most people already know. The other party perceives this as a sign that they are way to badass to have time to think about this or that.

EXAMPLE CONVERSATION #1

Friend: Did you hear that they finally caught that shooter?

Badass: There was a shooter?

Friend: Yeah, that crazy dude who killed all those people last week.

Badass: Aww, that sucks.

Friend: Yeah, what's the world coming to these days?

Badass: I don't know. I didn't even know there was a shooter. Again. For the millionth time. The news is garbage, stop wasting your life.

EXAMPLE CONVERSATION #2

Friend: I watched this documentary on dogs last night. Did you know that the dog has been domesticated thousands of years longer than any other animal?

Badass: I didn't know that

Friend: Yeah, what did you think it would be, the horse?

Badass: I have never asked myself that question.

Friend: It's just fun trivia.

Badass: Yeah, the thing is, I am super busy with all the stuff I do every day. No time for trivia I guess. I gotta go, this dude owes me money and he's out of warnings.

- Those example conversations I suppose could be a little misleading. The last line of each of those conversations are not words that the badass would actually say out loud. The last line is exactly the message that the badass is sending with their facial expression and body language. A real badass would never actually They carry themselves with humility, never ashamed to learn something new that most people already know. The other party will assume that you have been way too busy being a badass to care about a crazy shooter or a documentary. As far as they know, you might have been the person harboring the shooter all week, and your dog is actually pure-wolf and has eaten people.

> Badasses are actually very humble people, and this is why it is often not hard for them to admit their faults. They'll freely admit when they do not know something, they show genuine interest in other people. They make eye contact and they consider themselves in charge of the conversation. They may be listening to what you're telling them at the moment, but make no mistake, they are completely in charge of the direction this conversation takes. If you bore them with too much detail and start cutting into their turn to talk, they will often show signs of polite boredom. (<u>Polite boredom</u>: If they show an exagerrated emotional reaction to your child, cat, or dog walking in, they are politely bored.)

- A badass keeps a commanding body stance when necessary. Their regular pose might be curled up innocently perched barefoot on the couch, or kicking back with one foot up, whatever feels the most comfortable, and take note that a badass treats their own comfort as a serious matter. You could say that a civilized stance is all that separates the badass from the beast. Don't be fooled by the guy holding the door open for you at the store. He fits the profile of a undercover badass. Also, beware of the lady at the pharmacy with the million-dollar smile. Badasses are cosummate charmers.

- Badasses take risks. Foolish people take stupid risks, but badasses love a calculated risk that is likely to pay off. This includes something as simple as approaching a stranger in an unthreatening way so as to introduce themselves. The ones you know are probably frequently signing up for an adventure that requires them to meet a challenge.

- Like every other human being, badasses have their share of failures. The difference is in how a badass views failure. The average woman might feel rejected if a first date with a new crush didn't lead to a second date. The badass woman knows she is a catch and counts it a blessing that she probably avoided a future heartache or a series of dramatic excuses. The badass's time is too precious to waste on what *might have been* in an alternate reality. There is a real reality happening right now all the time with real people out there who will actually respect your time.

- When you're a badass, you celebrate your friends as frequently as possible. Go to their birthday parties if you're invited, attend their grandparent's funeral, buy them a thoughtful Christmas gift, remember their kids' ages, and when they accomplish something, anything at all, make a sincere effort to acknowledge it. It's this quality that gives the badass the solid core of close friends that make them the envy of others. They earn that loyalty, and they expect the same loyalty in return.

Decisive People: Just as Flawed, Ten Times Happier!

Do you remember Wembley from *Fraggle Rock*? He was pathologically indecisive, citing that if you say *yes* to one thing, you are also saying *no* to another. Decisions require some analyzing, but only when there is uncertainty in our gut.

A badass is decisive, from the gut. This is not my greatest strength, but I have to agree that I have noticed that pattern before. Indecisive people are much more prone to miss a good opportunity. If you take to long to weigh the pros and cons, it demonstrates that your analytical mind is more of a hindrance to your success than an asset.

If you struggle with being indecisive, you'll benefit from my 6-step approach to making quick decisions. There are usually underlying causes, and dealing with these later may help you conquer your fear of decisions. My approach deals with only the superficial aspect: achieving the illusion of being decisive while probably not making a bad choice. It's no substitute for every decision and should not be used for any choice that might have lasting conseuqences (think: tattoo), but my method will help you to control the anxiety you feel when you have to make a quick decision.

How to make a quick confident decision in a snap!
(using **S.T.A.R.R.Y.**)

S   Study up on the subject at hand. This is the best way to be prepared to make an informed decision. Unfortunately, we don't usually have an agenda listing the decisions we will be making tomorrow. In the case where you have no idea what to do and you have a minute or two, slip back a few steps and do a Google search for the exact scenario on your phone. (They will assume you are replying to an urgent text, so just let them assume. Don't lie, but it's really none of their business what you're doing.) Don't click on the first couple answers, they're almost always ads, go to a site where real people are sharing their actual opinions and their reasons. After reading opinions from both sides, you should have a much better handle on what will be the best decision for you. This should not take longer than 3 minutes.

T   Too many factors. Remind yourself that there will never be enough time to weigh all of the data when facing a choice. There are millions of factors affecting every detail all the time. So, why do some people seem so sure of themselves when making decisions? Sorry to ruin their illusion, but they are just using their best judgement, and they often have no reason to be any more confident than you.

A   Act as if you know exactly what you want. Use this only as a last resort. If it is taking longer than twenty seconds to pick an ice cream flavor, you need to just pick one and pretend it was the best choice you ever made. Badasses stick to their decision. Don't fall for the easy trap of blaming the ice cream parlor. If you hate the flavor you chose that badly, just go get a different one. "I guess I wasn't in the mood for Minty Macadamia Mango. I'm going to go ask for that vanilla I almost chose. You want the rest of this one?"

R   Recommendations are priceless. A good recommendation from an expert should carry a lot of weight, enough to potentially change your mind. If you need to make a quick decision, there's usually other people around who would gladly share their opinion with you. It's a better start than being clueless. Plus, you might also make a friend. "Excuse me, do you know what kind of mochaccinoiato I should get? I never come here."

R   Repeat someone who went before you. This might require some eavesdropping while someone is explaining it all to the poor sap who admitted he didn't know. This is the classic, "I'll have what she's having" technique.

Y   You genuinely don't care? This is an acceptable answer. You will forfeit the right to take credit later, but a badass is never short on praise, so as long as you really don't care, let someone who does care make the decision.

More Badass Class

- A badass focuses on what THEY want in life. Pleasing other people comes after you can show that you already know what YOU want. Now, tell me what you want—what you really, really want.
- Badasses **never give up** on pursuing what they want, ever.
- A badass never talks about being a badass, ever.
- Badasses maintain their composure even when things get crazy. The trick to this is to train your mind to approach any problem as the solver, never as a potential victim. A badass will never be complicit in their own victimization because they have completely ruled-out the option to play the victim. Even if they get ripped off, they may be angry, but they will remain calm because they know that nothing good comes from impulsive reactions. They will think it through, and when they have sorted out how they ended up with the short end of the stick, they will remedy the situation right away. Badasses don't get victimized, badasses don't overreact, and badasses don't want to waste time making a situation worse. If they can make it better, great, but not at the expense of their more important pursuits.
- Badasses do not get easily offended. You can call them names, make fun of their faults, and they will have a good laugh with you IF it is actually funny. They aren't aiming to seem perfect. Their goals are too tied directly to what they value, and badasses don't take humor personally.
- Badasses do not pick fights with others. That's a punk ass, also a dumbass, and is the opposite of a badass.
- Badasses do not hog the limelight. If it is someone else's time to shine, they remain a strong presence, but allow the attention to stay on others. A quiet respect for their moment will earn you more respect than drawing attention to yourself, and a badass feels no need to take any of the credit, although they are often given more than they actually deserve.
- Badasses know just the right time to be vulnerable. The Dirty Harry approach is not appropriate in all settings. If everyone is putting their hearts out on the table, the badass knows that revealing a little of their humanity is sometimes the best approach. It never hurts to put a little spin on it. For example, when recalling stupid things we did when we were young, I have to remember to end that memory with a quick review of what I learned from that experience. A badass owns a mistake once, but owns the lesson learned forever.

This is what the Urban Dictionary has to say:
bad ass
adj. 1. A general **term** used to describe behavior that is fearless, **authentic**, compassionate, and ethical. 2. Well above the social standard for "**normal**" behavior. 3. The opposite of dumb ass behavior.[1]

---

[1] https://www.urbandictionary.com/define.php?term=badass

"It isn't what you have or who you are or where you are or what you are doing that makes you happy or unhappy. It is what you think about it."
— Dale Carnegie, *How to Win Friends and Influence People*

Aim Toward Becoming the Baddest of Asses

1. Do what you love. This has been a highly-resonant message for me recently, and it led to a new and completely unexpected path of self-discovery. "Do what you love." For weeks I was seeing this message, and I knew it would all make sense when the time was right. Guess what? That all happened.

2. Approach this book with an open mind. I cannot change your years of negative self-talk without your full cooperation. Do the journal exercises, read at least some of this book daily, practice the strategies and then you will have laid a foundation for success. Your greatest enemy is faulty past thinking that has started to do more harm than good. If we are going to correct your thinking, it requires your effort. Like the old saying, "You'll only get out of it what you put into it." That quote directly applies to these badass behaviors.

3. Be willing to fail, as many times as necessary. It's just part of the human learning process. Everybody fails many times in a lifetime, even the most successful of us. The trick is to ta   p into your hidden tenacity, get up, start again, and reframe the whole situation as a learning experience. No regrets for trying. When people see us fail, they can relate. Everybody fails and they can empathize. When we rise again, we will naturally have an influence on those who are observing our climb back. Badasses don't want sympathy.

4. Be willing to work very hard. Louis Pasteur, the father of microbiology—a genius mind—said that even he credits his strength to simply not giving up.

   > **"Let me tell you the secret that has led me to my goals: my strength lies solely in my tenacity."**
   > **-- Louis Pasteur**

5. Remember that the learning process is a cycle that builds on itself. You try something, see how much of it comes naturally, integrate prior knowledge with your first attempt, and then formulate a more successful approach and a smarter stratey. Every time we attempt another try, we come at every challenge a lot faster and with greater accuracy. This is how we learned to walk, read, ride a bicycle, drive a car, and beat our favorite video game. We gave ourselves as many chances as we needed to succeed at those new skills, why would we start getting so impatient with ourselves after all these years of practice.

6. With time comes experience and wisdom. By about the age of thirty, we start to expect our behavior to be error-free. We claim to be adults, we are trusted to make serious decisions, and retaining new information comes easy, so we can tend to come down on ourselves pretty hard if we mess up. The truth is, we should never expect to reach a time when we stop making mistakes. Knowing this will help us find the courage to keep getting back up. It will also help us forgive those loved ones who keep letting us down. Maybe this lesson is going to take them their whole life, and they are coping with the frustration the best way they know how.

7. When you're called to help, always suit up and show up, and from now on do it in your own unique badass style.

8. Don't argue with others. A badass is above petty arguing. Right or wrong does not concern the badass as much as the art of making it clear that it won't phase them either way. (Wow, I was wrong all this time. Oh well. Even Jackie Robinson struck out every once in a while.) Avoid creating unecessary conflicts with other people. Getting into fights to prove you are a badass is not approved by this badass program. Yes, some people are great at fighting, and to a lot of people that is pretty

badass, but it doesn't take a genius to see how far fighting everyone will get you. That's more asinine than badass.

9. It's a hard pill to swallow if you have to admit that you don't trust your intuition, your gut. You have every reason in the world TO trust your gut, even if it is sometimes not perfectly accurate. "Intuition" is such a mysterious word, but really intuition is nothing more than the data from our combined senses filtered through all the life lessons and challenges that we have worked so hard to overcome. I use the word intuition to refer to your instincts that move you to behave a certain way based on the framework you've built in your mind. Your intuition should be your MOST trusted resource. It has been speculated by theologians that it is in our intuitive brain that God chooses to communicate directly with us. Some people call it the ability to read an entire situation and pick up on patterns and connections. Stop doubting yourself. You would be right more often than you will be wrong even if all you had was your intuition.

10. Fear, anxiety, excitement, anger, extreme joy, and surprise all get our heart pumping. Get your heart racing for a good reason as soon as you feel it starting to beat fast for a bad reason. Once you have trained your brain to see anxiety as excitement instead, you will notice your overall anxiety diminishing dramatically. You are well on your way to being your own badass.

11. The self-confidence part of the human behavior is directly attached to the hardware of the brain. Don't expect results without patient reprogramming.

12. Badasses don't waste time lying to themselves. If they messed up, they admit it and choose to remember the experience as a lesson instead of a mistake. They do not, however, go around saying that it was all a big success, when it clearly wasn't. It might all be a huge mess, but they don't exagerrate it either way.

13. Stop using dark humor to make light of problems. "I guess I am not as smart as I thought", "FML", "Why am I cursed to re-live this again and again?", "I guess all these problems will give me something to do while I wait to die."

14. A badass builds up other peoples' confidence. You can say a bunch of mean things to a very confident person, and if you hit a certain nerve, you can really weaken their confidence. That would be a misuse of perspective shifting. The right way to use it is constructively, and it works using the same principles. You can make the most insecure person feel a permanent increase in their self-esteem with the right advice too.

Your Unique Brand of Badass

What else are you? Below are a list of personality traits and characteristics that you might have displayed before in your life. Look over the list below. Circle ANY trait or characteristic that you have EVER used to your advantage. Highlight the ones you use frequently. This is your unique brand of badass at a glance. As you recall more, return to this page and circle the characteristic:

Accountable	Adaptable	Adventure
Alert	Ambitious	Appropriate
Assertive	Clever	Attentive
Authentic	Aware	Brave
Tranquil	Candid	Capable
Certain	Charismatic	Caring
Collaborative	Committed	Communicator
Compassionate	Trustworthy friend	Connected
Conscious	Considerate	Consistent
Contributes	Cooperative	Courageous
Creativity	Curiosity	Dedicated
Determination	Diplomatic	Directive
Discipline	Dynamic	Easy-going
Effectiveness	Efficient	Empathy
Empowered Self	Energetic	Enthusiasm
Ethical Values	Ever-evolving	Expressive
Reassuring	Fairness	Faithful
Fearless	Flexible	Friendly
Generative	Generosity	Grateful
Happy	Hard Working	Honest
Honorable	Witty	Imaginative
Deep thinker	Independent	Gets things going
Innovative	Inquiring	Asks questions
Integrates	Integrity	Intelligent
Intentional	Interested	Personable
Joyful	Knowledgeable	Leading
Listener	Lively	Logical
Loving	Loyal	Time Management
Networker	Nurturing	Open-Minded
Optimistic	Organized	Patient
Peaceful	Planner	Playful
Poised	Polite	Powerful
Practical	Well-mannered	Proactive
Problem-Solver	Productive	Punctual
Reliable	Resourceful	Responsible
Self-confident	Self-motivating	Self-reliant
Funny	Appreciative	Serves Others
Sincere	Skillful	Spiritual
Spontaneous	Stable	Strong
Goal-oriented	Supportive	Tactful
Trusting	Trustworthy	Truthful
Versatile	Vibrant	Warm/loving
Willing	Intuitive	Zealous

Don't Let the Pine Trees Blow Your Mind, Please

Don't let Christmas-y stuff get to you. Think of it the way you would if you saw all of the residents of some foreign village putting up decorations that correlate with their seasonal festivals. Here are some tips to keep you from getting too agitated during the holidays:

1. Don't be alone, unless you really, really want to.

2. Use moderation if you're using intoxicants. Avoid them if you can't moderate.

3. Don't stop your regular routine.

4. Express your feelings to a trusted person.

5. Try taking up a new interest. There are a million ideas out there, just Google: "Ideas for new hobbies or interests"

6. If things get really bad, there are people you can call:

1-800-273-TALK The National Suicide Prevention Lifeline

741741   The Crisis Text Line (simply send a text message to 741741)

https://www.thetrevorproject.org/ is a crisis site with safe on-line resources for depressed LGBT youth ages 13-24

https://www.hopeline-nc.org/ is an excellent resource for any kind of crisis.
CALL OR TEXT: 919-231-4525 | 1-877-235-4525

There is also a prayer line, if you are spiritually inclined, that I would recommend. I have used this one myself, and I am pleasantly surprised by their calm, non-judgmental demeanor every time. I will also include their website for other resources that have a spiritual approach:
Silent Unity
Call: 1-800-NOW-PRAY (669-7729)
International: 01-816-969-2000
http://www.unity.org/prayer

Stop Panicking at the Disco!

Use your journal as a tool for getting out of a panic attack immediately. While you are re-framing your mistakes as lessons learned, start re-framing all anxiety you feel as a manifestation of excitement for living your life. You might be surprised to know that the same physiological reaction happens whether we are panicking or just really excited about something. Anxiety is actually not a difficult emotion to re-frame, it just requires that you notice the signs of panic early, and quickly engage in an exciting activity, such as running around the block with your child, rolling around on the floor, or blasting a bass-driven track that is dripping with profanity. Get your heart pumping for a good reason, and your panic attacks will become obsolete. In fact, once you have trained your brain to see anxiety as excitement instead, you will probably notice your overall anxiety diminishing dramatically.

<u>Anxiety-Neutralizing Activities (put that elevated heart rate to good use):</u>

Vacuum
Clean the hard-to-reach windows
Toss a football with your child
Dust
Clean the garage
Run in place for three minutes
Mow the lawn
Pull weeds
Couch cushions = punching bag
Bathe the dog
Trim the trees
Clean the refrigerator
Clean the bathtub
Go check the mail
Call your most annoying relative
Move furniture around
Change your bed sheets
Clean the closet

Journal Update

("How I Will Deal With My Next Anxiety Attack")

Find a nice blank page in your journal and title it, "How I Will Deal With My Next Anxiety Attack" and then give yourself a few activity options that you will be ready to dive into as soon as you notice the anxiety wave coming in.

More Holiday Survival Tips

- Let nature snap you back into reality.
  - o hike, walk a dog, do some gardening
  - o watch the sun come up, or watch it go down
  - o walk to a nearby friend's house and bring them a plate of cookies

- Get creative
  - o paint, take pictures, draw, sculpt
  - o write a poem or a short story
  - o read a classic

- Pamper yourself
  - o bubble bath
  - o get a haircut
  - o treat yourself to a massage
  - o start a new healthy habit that sounds fun

- Flex your brain
  - o Pick a subject that fascinates you and watch a documentary on YouTube
  - o Enroll in an on-line class
  - o Read a non-fiction book about an subject you love

- Keep busy
  - o Start a project
  - o Plan a party
  - o Clean the house
  - o Donate old clothes to charity
  - o Throw yourself into a task you've been procrastinating

Reclaiming Your Now. Now.

The fastest way to get us back in the confident now is by establishing a *confidence now cue*. I prefer using a playlist I create of songs to get me moving and reignite any neglected motivation. I will not tell you what embarrassing anthems I draw inspiration from because I want your mind to be clear when you attempt the next mental activity. This will be fun: List everything you can think of that inspires you. Think movies, songs, soundtracks, a particular genre, a motivational speaker (there's a huge selection on YouTube), your ex's sports jersey, or a big pancake breakfast. Whatever moves you, whatever drives you, whatever wakes up that warrior within, list them in your journal. Use the following chart as a guide if it helps.

3 Movies that inspire me:	3 People I know, or who I have met, who inspire me:
1. 2. 3.	1. 2. 3.
5 Famous people who inspire me to work hard:	**The 5 most Beautiful places in the world:**
1. 2. 3. 4.	1. 2. 3. 4.

5.	**5.**
3 Activities that make me smile the biggest:	**3 Surprises I would love to have happen right now:**
1. **2.** **3.**	**1.** **2.** **3.**
3 Big projects I would undertake if I had 10 billion dollars (not including a shopping spree):	**3 Things I would tell a 5-year-old if they asked, "What makes life worth living?"**
1. **2.** **3.**	**1.** **2.** **3.**
7 Songs that make driving (or housework) fun:	**7 Songs that make me feel sexy or powerful:**
1. **2.**	**1.** **2.**

3. 4. 5. 6. 7.	3. 4. 5. 6. 7.
3 People I would love to meet:	**3 foods that feel like rewards:**
1. 2. 3.	1. 2. 3.

Journal Update

<u>**My Emergency Motivational Resource List**</u>

Somewhere near the front of your journal, keep a list of things that motivate you, such as songs, movies, or a favorite motivational speaker's pep talk. This list may be just the thing you need to drag yourself out of bed one day.

Inspiration for Motivational Elevation

That guide must have inspired a few ideas to get you up and create a motivation plan in your journal.

For those of us who just can't even try to be creative right now, there is an album I stumbled across on Spotify one day. It is the best mash-up of motivational speech excerpts I have ever heard.

Although I have no vested interest in the album and had no hand in creating it, I must insist that you find it on Spotify or buy the digital album on Amazon (hyper-linked below). It will be a very wise investment. I don't know where this brilliant gem has been hiding all my life. You must hear this entire album. I have listened to the entire album at least a dozen times, and it still gets my mind on the right track every time. *If you are reading this on your Kindle, I have provided hyperlinks below.*

Motivation for Overcoming Depression   --- Click Here to be directed to album
WakeUpTime

One of the speakers featured on this album is Alan Watts, the acclaimed lecturer and author, and it is an excerpt from a longer lecture during which he draws many connections between ancient eastern philosophies and modern man's struggle for a sense of purpose. I am including an excerpt from a collection of his essays. The book is called *Become What You Are*. See how he uses the eastern concepts of Yin/Yang, meditation, and the wheel of life to bring us back to the Now:

> "Almost every fundamental principle of life can be expressed in two opposite ways. There are those who say that to attain the highest wisdom we must be still and calm, immovable in the midst of turmoil. And there are those who say that we must move on as life moves, never stopping for a moment either in fear of what is to come or to turn a regretful glance at what has gone. The former are as those who listen to music, letting the flow of notes pass through their minds without trying either to arrest them or to speed them on. Like Chuang-Tzu's perfect man, they employ their minds as a mirror: it grasps nothing; it refuses nothing; it receives, but does not keep. The latter are as those who dance to music, keeping pace with its movement and letting their limbs flow with it as unceasingly and as unhesitatingly as clouds respond to the breath of wind. The one seems

to reflect events as they pass, and the other to move forward with them. Both points of view, however, are true, for to attain that highest wisdom we must at once walk on and remain still. Consider life as a revolving wheel set upright with man walking on its tire. As he walks, the wheel is revolving toward him beneath his feet, and if he is not to be carried backward by it and flung to the ground he must walk at the same speed as the wheel turns. If he exceeds that speed, he will topple forward and slip off the wheel onto his face. For at every moment we stand, as it were, on the top of a wheel; immediately we try to cling to that moment, to that particular point of the wheel, it is no longer at the top and we are off our balance. Thus by not trying to seize the moment, we keep it, for the second we fail to walk on we cease to remain still. Yet within this there is a still deeper truth. From the standpoint of eternity we never can and never do leave the top of the wheel, for if a circle is set in infinite space it has neither top nor bottom. Wherever you stand is the top, and it revolves only because you are pushing it round with your own feet."
— **Alan W. Watts**, *Become What You Are*

In this selection, Watts is referring to the Wheel of Life, which was first described in the ancient Hindu scriptures over 3,500 years ago. This wheel is described as endlessly turning between time and space.

This description reminds me of the way some of us view our past. Have you ever caught yourself reflecting on the past and it seems like all life has ever been is a series of mistakes. We may cringe while thinking about the past because we think there is something to run from. The good news is, there is nothing in your past that you need to distance yourself from and the only ghosts from your mistakes that will haunt you are the nightmares you conjure. If you can break free from the bonds of time, you will be free from delusion. The most deceptive prison we face is made of stone, metal, and time. If you have truly been freed from delusional thinking, you have attained the highest goal.2

What does it mean to break free from the bonds of time? You will need to break the power that the past, which only exists in the human mind, has over your mood. There are ways to achieve an illusion of beating time, but there is only one guaranteed way to beat time for real. Take back any power you have let the choices of yesterday to hold over us today. Regret will fester and cause all manners of illness and mental anguish. Let go of the past, and don't dwell too much on the future. The metaphor of the wheel of time is a teaching tool. It allowed the ancients to understand the unique nature of space-time thousands of years before Einstein put it into a scientific theory. It has not gone unnoticed that Einstein's theories on time and space have several very obvious similarities to the ancient Hindu texts. They both claim that space and time are not absolute, and that energy and matter are fundamentally the same. We have been using fire for eons to turn matter into energy, and only recently have scientists been on the track to create matter from energy. Similar experiments have been successful, but only recently have scientists been able to create a very small amount of matter out of energy alone. The long-term impact of this mind-bending technology will be nothing short of revolutionary.3

So, why the random lesson on Einstein's theories of pace-time and Hinduism? I want you to see that the manner in which events unfold may seem like a typical day to us, but it really is quite magical if you learn the proper perspective. Because time is a very unique force in the universe, it has very special characteristics. The best and worst one is this: Once an event has been played out in time, it will immediately begin to disappear. We know this because as a species we are always trying to hold on to the past. We try to fight against time, but it is no use.

---

2 From the Hindu Ashramas, circa 1,500 B.C.
3 Forbes https://www.forbes.com/sites/paulrodgers/2014/05/19/einstein-was-right-you-can-turn-energy-into-matter/#4fb058ff26ac

The past is irretrievable, for everybody, including all mistakes and horrors. The present moment is a white board that is constantly wiping away the old to make room for the new. There is absolutely no reason to get bogged down with regret about the past because, by nature, the past is gone forever.

Walk on a quick path with me through a beautiful forest. If I told you that there used to be saber-toothed tigers in this forest, would you start looking in the forest for them? If I explained that they have been extinct for about 11,000 years, would you still look out for one? Probably not. They are gone, leaving only fragments as proof they ever lived, and extinct animals are irretrievable. We don't miss them, we don't fear them, and we do not waste mental time thinking too much about them. In no way do they identify us. Why? Because they are in the past only, meaning they no longer exist.

The past DOES NOT EXIST so stop letting those memories steal your energy from focusing on what you want in life RIGHT NOW. Good memories, bad memories, regret, grief, joy, and missed opportunities… They all distract us from RIGHT NOW. It's like a never-ending Facebook newsfeed in the brain that tricks us into scrolling down a mental rabbit hole.

Badasses don't need mental rabbit holes, they would rather take advantage of the real Wonderland all around them.

"The very least you can do in your life is figure out what you hope for. And the most you can do is live inside that hope. Not admire it from a distance but live right in it, under its roof."
— Barbara Kingsolver, *Animal Dreams*

Journal Update

Don't forget to update your gratitude list regularly!

Non-Traditional Ways to Spend December 25th

- Go fishing.
- Go to the gym.
- Visit your Jehovah's Witness friends.
- Be tolerant of those who love Christmas.
- Make a song playlist that YOU love.
- Go out to a new movie.
- Write out cards to friends and family that tell them how much you love and appreciate them, stamp them, have them all ready to be mailed after January 1st. Pick a very non-Christmas theme, like a tropical island. (If you don't have that many friends, then write the same friend twelve times, one for each month of the next year).
- Make it the day you always clean your house and fill up your car with donations for the poor.
- Paint a picture.
- Make up your own activity. What makes you happy? The store doesn't have to be open to have fun. Write your ideas here:

  - _______________________________________
  - _______________________________________
  - _______________________________________
  - _______________________________________
  - _______________________________________
  - _______________________________________
  - _______________________________________

What You Need to Hear Every Day from Now On

I have filled the last pages of the book with motivational reminders. Read them everyday, and please feel free to photocopy any of these and post them all over your house. Copy extras for any friends that might need a little boost as well.

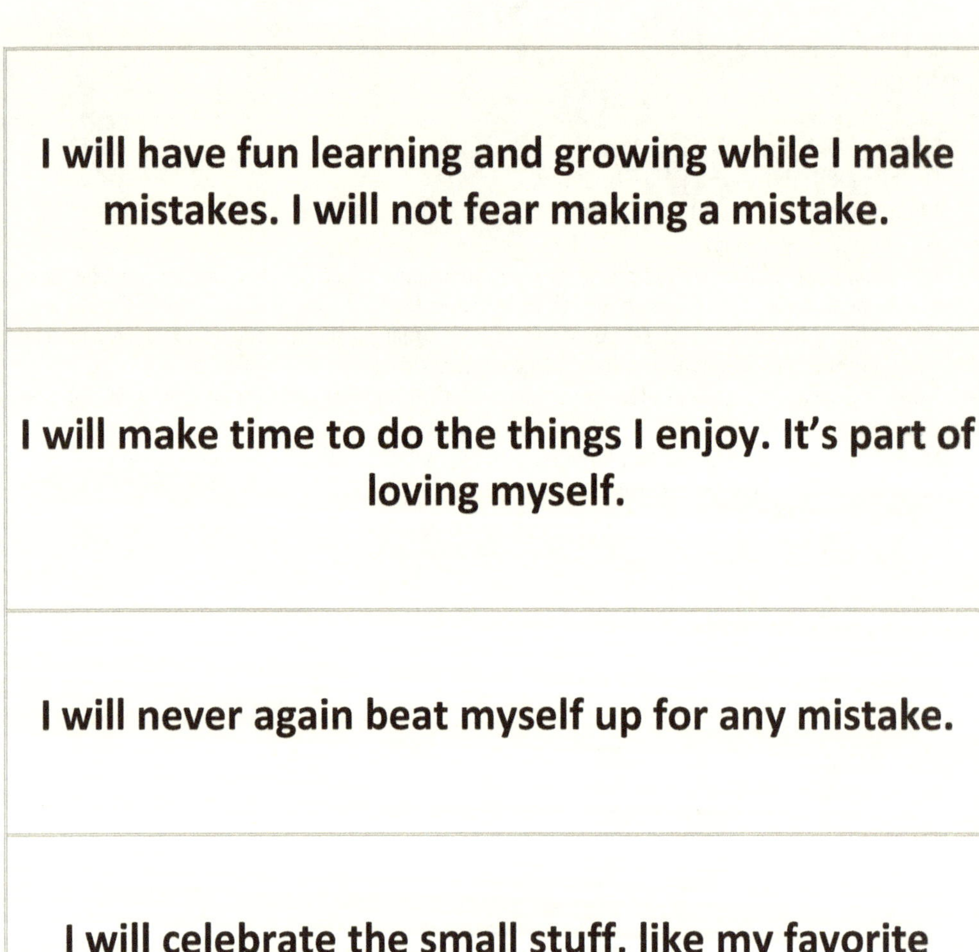

I will celebrate the small stuff, like my favorite meal and time with my dog.

I will surround myself with supportive people.

I deserve to be happy and confident as much as anyone else.

Feeling good about myself is not selfish, it is my responsibility as a human being.

Free Except from My Next Badass Book (Read These Every Day)

I am working on a Badass affirmation picture book. Here is a preview:

Self-love
is not
conditional.

I will discover what I

am passionate about,

and I will do that.

I will

let go

of

past crap.

I am not ashamed
of my imperfections.

I will

trust

my instincts.

Comparing myself to

others is stupid,

so I don't.

I will not

criticize

myself.

Ever.

Thank you for reading!

(Click here to
be directed to
my Amazon store)